Gabriel Fogarty-Graveson
& Felix Grainger

Sniff

Salamander Street

PLAYS

First published in 2024 by Salamander Street Ltd., a Wordville imprint. (info@salamanderstreetcom).

Sniff © Gabriel Fogarty-Graveson & Felix Grainger, 2024

Cover Image: Oisín Tammas.

PB ISBN: 9781738429356

10 9 8 7 6 5 4 3 2 1

Further copies of this publication can be purchased from www.salamanderstreet.com

Wordville

INTRODUCTION

Sniff has been a passion project that I began working on about three years ago. It was originally a Hertfordshire-based story—one very close to my heart.

I had just graduated from drama school and then, boom, Covid hit. I—like many others—was stuck back in my home county, and was left to my own brain and thoughts. Everything around me reminded me of being a kid growing up. The parks, the pubs, the bike rides, the football—although many of these we weren't actually allowed to enjoy at this point. But, as the months went on, and the lockdowns were lifted, I could feel myself reconnecting with the place that birthed me, and the friends I'd grown up with.

Coming from a small city with a strong group of mates, I have witnessed how different paths in life can drastically change people's experiences of the world. Those who went to uni, those who got a job straight after school, those who left home, and those who didn't. When you're young, these differences don't mean much—you're all gonna end up at the same house party on a Friday night after all. But when you look back, those small differences can really change the path of a person's life. With this in mind, I began writing the character of Liam. A friend of mine, Joe O'Shea—a film-maker, accompanied me to a random car park, and he filmed me doing a performance of it to camera. This was the first ever rendition of *Sniff*.

I loved the character of Liam. I was obsessed by his optimism, despite his difficult situation. I felt like I understood him. But I knew I wanted to turn it into something bigger. So, when OVO Theatre Company was looking for new-writing plays, I turned to my writing partner and one of the co-founders of Make It Beautiful Theatre Company: Felix Grainger. Together, with the help of the director Ben Purkiss, we used improvisation and a long R&D process to create a version of *Sniff* that is much more similar to what it is now. Most importantly, the role of Alex was born.

Liam and Alex—for me—are both the antithesis of each other, whilst also being somewhat similar. They represent different paths and disparate realities—but are either of them happy? The aim of *Sniff* was always to show the complexities of these characters. For instance, another important element of the show is addiction (in its various forms) and how it can both bring short-term meaning and euphoria, but then inevitably just as quickly take those feelings away. These substances and these habits are nuanced—as much as people may not like to think so.

After a successful scratch performance at the Maltings Theatre in St Albans, we were then fortunately chosen by Theatre503—a London space dedicated to honing new-writing—to perform there in 2022. The more Felix and I performed the play, the more we learnt about the characters and the story. It forced us to make edits, rethink, re-structure. It was a bit of a chaotic way of writing a final draft—but it felt oddly right. Like we had to live the experiences of Liam and Alex to find the ultimate truth.

In 2023, we performed a newer version of *Sniff* at the Jack Studio Theatre in Brockley. This was the longest run we'd done, and probably the last run we thought we'd ever do. The show felt finished, and we'd received some really positive feedback. We also had other projects with the company that we wanted to focus on, as well as our own solo creative careers. However, as is the way with *Sniff*, it managed to find its way back into our lives. The character of Liam, and the story of him in that toilet, tugged on my arm once again.

I had just finished studying at the Philippe Gaulier clown school, and Felix was deep into a UK theatre tour, when the Park Theatre offered us the opportunity to perform our final, evolved version of *Sniff* at their incredible space. Like The Avengers, Felix, Ben and I reconvened and decided that the story needed to be told again. After another process of R&D, we had our final version of *Sniff* ready to be performed at the Park in 2024. We were also thrilled that Salamander Street would be publishing it.

The story of *Sniff* is one that many, we hope, will relate to. We all know a Liam, and we all know an Alex. After watching the play, I want people to ask themselves the question: who would you rather be? Liam or Alex? Because, personally, I genuinely don't know.

This play is an ode to the forgotten souls who try so desperately to stay in the beautiful, innocent and euphoric youthful years that encapsulated a much, much simpler time.

Gabriel Fogarty-Graveson
2024

ACKNOWLEDGEMENTS

There were many people who helped create *Sniff* into what it is now. Thank you all:

Park Theatre

OVO Theatre

Theatre503

Jack Studio Theatre

Ben Purkiss

Oisín Tammas

Lucy George

Salamander Street

The STA boys

Louis Tambala

Joe O'Shea

Oliver Adams—for your optimism, help and loving friendship

Sniff was first developed and performed at the Maltings Theatre in St Albans in March 2022. It was then selected as an 'outstanding' script by Theatre503 and performed there in July 2022. It then went on to a longer run at the Jack Studio in February 2023, and then the Park Theatre in May 2024.

CAST

Liam:	**Gabriel Fogarty-Graveson**
Alex:	**Felix Grainger**
Bloke:	**Ben Purkiss / Alfie Snow**

CREATIVES

Writers:	**Gabriel Fogarty-Graveson & Felix Grainger**
Director:	**Ben Purkiss**
Producer:	**Make It Beautiful Theatre Company**
Composer/Sound Designer:	**Louis Tambala**

ABOUT THE CAST AND CREATIVES

Gabriel Fogarty-Graveson | Actor & Playwright

Gabriel is an actor, writer and theatre-maker born in Hertfordshire. He trained at the University of East Anglia, Drama Centre London, the Boris Shchukin Theatre Institute in Moscow and at the Philippe Gaulier school in France. He is one of the co-founders of Make It Beautiful Theatre Company. His acting and writing credits include: *The CO-OP* at Park Theatre and English Theatre of Hamburg, *The Hanging Gibbet* at the Norwich Theatre, *Our Little Life* at the Black Box Studio in Slovenia. In 2023, he appeared as Laurie in a tour of *Little Women*, as well as Connor in *The Nag's Head* at Park Theatre. He also starred in the British Short Film Award Shortlisted film *Bugbear*, and played Billy in the 2024 short-film *Back of the Net*. Gabriel is one of the co-writers of *Sniff*.

Felix Grainger| Actor & Playwright

From Shropshire, Felix studied psychology before training as an actor at Drama Centre London. He co-founded Make it Beautiful Theatre Company straight out of drama school and was also a member of Shake it Up, the improvised Shakespeare company, as well as starring in the world premiere of Peter Whelan's *Sleepers in the Field* at Questors. Felix played Romeo with Dickens Theatre Company (New Wimbledon Theatre, Aylesbury Waterside, ATG main house tour), The Porter in *Macbeth* and Robert Louis Stevenson/Inspector Newcomen in *Jekyll and Hyde* (UK Tour) and as a writer and actor with Make it Beautiful Theatre Company he has starred/written in *The CO-OP, Our Little Life, The Dream Machine, Severn Stories* and *The Nag's Head*. Felix is also one of the writers of *Sniff*.

Ben Purkiss | Director

Born and bred in London, Ben studied English and Drama at the
University of East Anglia where he discovered his passion for directing.
He has collaborated frequently as a freelance director with multiple
companies in London, including Little Lion Theatre and Make It
Beautiful. Ben also Assistant Directed Tramshed's community production
of *Jam Tomorrow*. These include working on *Our Little Life* at the Black Box
Studio in Slovenia, as well as various short plays. Ben has directed *Sniff*
through all of its previous performances and helped to develop the script
from its original concept.

Make It Beautiful Theatre Company | Producer

A London-based theatre company derived from the Drama Centre.
They are dedicated to magical storytelling, long-form improvisation,
comedy and unearthing the beautiful. Since 2019, the company has
been committed to telling and creating stories for UK and European
stages. They have collaborated and performed with a series of theatres,
including: the Park, the English Theatre of Hamburg, the Black Box
Studio of Slovenia, the Au Brana Cultural Centre in France, the Norwich
Theatre and a range of other London venues. *Sniff* is a project that
Make It Beautiful has been producing for many years, and perfectly
encapsulates the type of work they want to make.

www.makeitbeautiful.uk

TAMBALA | Composer & Sound Designer

Louis Tambala (TAMBALA) is a London-based electronic music producer.
TAMBALA's musical palette spans alternative R&B/rap, lo-fi, UK garage,
and everything in between. His solo productions and collaborative
tracks—with a diverse range of UK and US-based rappers and singers—
have accumulated millions of streams, showcasing his versatility and
unique approach to music-making. TAMBALA is recognised for adding
his unique creative touch to every track, using sampling and audio
manipulation to push boundaries and turn the ordinary into something
extraordinary.

PARK THEATRE

ABOUT PARK THEATRE

Park Theatre was founded by Artistic Director, Jez Bond and Creative Director Emeritus, Melli Marie. The building opened in May 2013 and, with nine West End transfers, two National Theatre transfers and 15 national tours in its first ten years, quickly garnered a reputation as a key player in the London theatrical scene. Park Theatre has received seven Olivier nominations, won numerous Off West End Offie Awards, and won The Stage's Fringe Theatre of the Year and Accessible Theatre Award.

Park Theatre is an inviting and accessible venue, delivering work of exceptional calibre in the heart of Finsbury Park. We work with writers, directors and designers of the highest quality to present compelling, exciting and beautifully told stories across our two intimate spaces.

Our programme encompasses a broad range of work from classics to revivals with a healthy dose of new writing, producing in-house as well as working in partnership with emerging and established producers. We strive to play our part within the UK's theatre ecology by offering mentoring, support and opportunities to artists and producers within a professional theatre-making environment.

Our Creative Engagement strategy seeks to widen the number and range of people who participate in theatre, and provides opportunities for those with little or no prior contact with the arts.

In everything we do we aim to be warm and inclusive; a safe, welcoming and wonderful space in which to work, create and visit.

★★★★★ "A five-star neighbourhood theatre." Independent

As a registered charity [number 1137223] with no public subsidy, we rely on the kind support of our donors and volunteers. To find out how you can get involved visit parktheatre.co.uk

FOR PARK THEATRE

Artistic Director Jez Bond
Executive Director Catherine McKinney

Creative Engagement

Creative Engagement Manager Carys Rose Thomas

Development

Head of Development Ama Ofori-Darko
Development & Producing Coordinator Ellen Harris

Finance

Finance Director Elaine Lavelle
Finance Officer Nicola Brown
Finance Assistant Pinar Kurdik

General Management

General Manager Tom Bailey
Deputy General Manager David Hunter
Producer Programmer Amelia Cherry
Administrator Mariah Sayer
Access Coordinator David Deacon
Duty Venue Managers Leiran Gibson, Zara Naeem, Laura Riseborough, Shaun Joyson, Wayne Morris

Park Pizza

Supervisor Jahmar Bennett
Park Pizza & Bar Team George Gehm, John Burman, Bradly Doko, Hugo Harrison, Alex Kristoffy, Julia Skinner, Maddie Stoneman, Eliyas Swart, Sion Watkins, Jessie Williams, Maria Ziolkowska

Gabriel Fogarty-Graveson
& Felix Grainger

Sniff

"To -3, to Clarence, to the Horn"

CHARACTERS

ALEX

LIAM

BLOKE

GRANDAD
(Liam's grandfather)

FATHER
(Alex's father)

DAD
(Liam's father)

MR PREECE
(Alex's boss)

NOTES ON THE PLAY

This play can be performed by a cast of up to seven actors, however, for this production *Sniff* is performed predominantly by two actors, playing Liam and Alex. The flashback scenes are multi-rolled by them, to ensure the claustrophobic world of the toilet is felt. A change of lighting, character choices and relationship to set is how the audience knows we are now in a different time and space. The only other character is Bloke, who is played by one other actor.

SCENE 1

The stage is dark. We hear the 'More Than A Woman' remix by Tambala. The light flickers.

We see the image of LIAM, holding a beer bottle over his head; panting, sweating, dishevelled.

Black out.

We hear the audio of a Bet Time Advertisement.

Snoring sound.

ADVERT V/O: Are you tired of work?
Are you tired of life?
Are you tired of feeling tired?
Well, it's time to wake up. (*echoes*)
That's right, It's not bedtime. It's Bet Time... With a T.
With Bet Time's super easy-to-use interface you can bet on anything at any time. Bet Time. (*echoes*) Bet on the football. Bet on the basketball. Bet on the rugby ball. You can bet in-play, out of play, any kind of play you like. Wondering how many seconds this advert will last? Well, there's a bet for that too. We make it all possible. Because isn't life that little bit more exciting when there's something to win and you've nothing to lose? So come on. Wake up. It's Bet Time.

Bet Time... (*sung*) More than a woman, more than a woman to me.

Lights up. A grim gents toilet in a pub. There's only one urinal, one cubicle and one sink. The cubicle has an 'Out of Order' sign on it. It is covered in graffiti and hilariously unfunny tags. On the walls are a variety of tribute band posters.

ALEX enters. He looks smart, dressed in a suit and cravat. He looks anxious. He notices the cubicle 'Out of Order' sign, so instead runs over to the urinal. He struggles to piss so begins humming 'More Than A Woman' by the BeeGees to himself.

Suddenly, LIAM's voice is heard from the cubicle.

LIAM: (*singing*) ... 'More than a woman...'

ALEX stops humming, and instantly becomes tense. He stays at the urinal.

...'More than a woman to me.'

LIAM, dressed much more casually than ALEX, comes out of the cubicle holding a bottle of beer. He goes to the sink and washes his hands. He looks in the mirror, steadies himself, and does a key of coke. He looks like Popeye when he gets his fix of spinach. LIAM watches ALEX.

ALEX continues to try and force out a piss.

LIAM: What's with the price of pints these days, eh? That's why I drink this. Only £2.99 from the corner shop and it still does the job.

He nods at his beer. ALEX ignores him.

My mate John, he lives in London, he told me he once went Kings Cross and paid £9 for a pint of Carling. Modern day mugging that. £9. I mean that's, what? Three meal deals? Tuna sandwich, diet coke and a packet of salt 'n' vinegar.

LIAM looks back into the mirror. He sings again.

'More than a woman'... They were all ugly bastards to be fair.

(Beat.)

The Gibbs. The Gibbatrons. The Studio Gibblys.

ALEX: Sorry, are you talking to me?

LIAM: Yeah... I was just saying that the Bee Gees are all ugly pricks.

ALEX: Bastards.

LIAM: What?

ALEX: You said 'bastards' not 'pricks'

(Beat.)

3

LIAM: Who holds the Guinness World Record for the longest ever piss? Cos whoever it is, I reckon you're about to ruin their day.

ALEX: I'm obviously not pissing. I can't piss. I can't piss in front of people. I get...

LIAM: Nervous?

ALEX doesn't respond.

Do you want me to turn the taps on?

ALEX: What? No.

LIAM gets a cigarette out and puts it in his mouth.

LIAM: It might help. Running water usually does. Or I can speak about the sea... or make whale sounds or something.

LIAM attempts to make the sound of a whale.

ALEX: Can you not/

LIAM: Make whale sounds?/

ALEX: Smoke in here.

(Beat.)

LIAM: So, you like the whale sounds?

ALEX: You shouldn't smoke in here.

LIAM: Why?

ALEX: It isn't allowed.

LIAM: Since when?

ALEX: Since when has smoking inside pubs not been allowed?

(Pause.)

Like 2007.

LIAM: Oh well. Who's counting?

ALEX: It's a well-known law.

LIAM: Alright. What are you? The Judge, Judy and Executor?

ALEX: What?

LIAM puts his cigarette away.

LIAM: Is it because your dick is small?

ALEX: Sorry?

LIAM: Is that why you can't piss in front of people? Cos honestly if it ain't small then what are you actually worried about?

(Beat.)

And even if it is small, who cares? Size doesn't correlate with sexual talent.

(Beat.)

My mate once made a girl orgasm just by looking at her intently, and everyone knows his dick looked like a sad prawn.

LIAM walks over to ALEX.

Do you want me to have a look?

ALEX: Back off, man!

LIAM: Alright.

LIAM steps back.

ALEX: It's not about it being small... OK? It's normal-sized. If anything, it's actually bigger than normal because of this enlarged vein on the side, which is also very, very normal. What it's really about, is not feeling comfortable enough to release the piss out of my normally sized phallus, in front of some... random.

LIAM: Some random?

ALEX: Yeah.

LIAM: Harsh.

ALEX: Why is that harsh?

LIAM: I'm not 'some random'. We know each other.

ALEX quickly scans LIAM.

ALEX: Do we?

LIAM: Yeah. We've spoken before. Loads actually. Remember?

ALEX: Obviously not because we've never met.

(Pause.)

LIAM: We did double science together in Year 9.

ALEX: No we didn't.

LIAM: Yeah we did, Mr Chapman's class, come on!

ALEX: I didn't even go to school here.

LIAM: Not sure, mate. Think we was definitely in Biology
together at least. You and me by the Bunsen Burners.

ALEX: No.

LIAM: I used to always say I had a crush on your sister.

ALEX: I don't have a sister.

LIAM: That's what you'd always say back then too!

ALEX: Stop it.

LIAM: Oh. It was a simpler time, weren't it?

ALEX: I have never seen you in my life.

(Beat.)

LIAM: You sure?

ALEX: Certain.

LIAM: 100%?

ALEX: 100%.

(Beat.)

LIAM: Maybe... maybe you're right. Maybe it was someone else.

ALEX: It was someone else. I've never even been to this weird town before.

LIAM: It's technically a city. We've got a cathedral, which means something apparently.

ALEX: As I said, I've never been here before.

LIAM: Ah well, you're one of the lucky ones. "Run. Run while you have the chance!"

LIAM points an imaginary gun at ALEX.

ALEX: What are you talking about?

LIAM: You pissed yet? I can't really piss until you do so.

ALEX: What's wrong with the cubicle?

LIAM: Wow. OK, you definitely don't live here. That toilet's been blocked since England lost to Italy on pens. And I ain't talking 2021, I'm talking 2012.

ALEX: You're telling me that no one has used that toilet for over 10 years?

LIAM looks at the cubicle.

LIAM: : Nah, nah... I use it. But more as storage... a sort of beer cooler, if you will.

ALEX: That's revolting.

LIAM: It keeps the bottles fresh. I'll stock it up at the beginning of the week with cheap, cornershop beer. Then I come in here, drink a bottle, go out there. It's a simple transaction. Want some?

LIAM offers ALEX the beer he's been drinking

ALEX: Listen… As much as I'd *love* to stay here and drink toilet lager with you, and reminisce about the supposed Bunsen burner days, when you had a crush on my imaginary sister… I actually really do have to get on with this piss and then get on with, you know, the rest of my life.

LIAM: Suit yourself.

LIAM does another key of coke. He snorts loudly. ALEX tries to piss again. He tenses up, squeezing everything. He then sighs.

ALEX: Bugger it. I can't piss under these conditions. I'm just gonna have to use the cubicle.

ALEX moves towards the cubicle. LIAM blocks his way.

LIAM: Nah, nah mate you really don't want to go in there. It's bad… really bad… It's the Hiroshima of toilets. It's like modern art. Like an explosion at Willy Wonka's chocolate factory, except all the chocolate is, well you know, poo.

ALEX takes this image in.

ALEX: Jesus christ. Alright. Fine. Turn those taps on.

LIAM: Now we're talking. Whale sounds?

ALEX: Please no.

LIAM turns the taps on and begins making whale sounds. ALEX suddenly feels like he may be able to release himself.

Hang on.. It's coming! It's coming! The whale sounds are working!

LIAM: I told you, mate.

ALEX: It's almost there.

LIAM: (*sung*) 'More than a woman'. All together now!

BOTH: (*sung*) 'More than a woman to me'…

Suddenly, the bathroom door swings open. A random BLOKE walks in, he is a dominating presence. Alex stops singing and quickly freezes up once again.

LIAM looks at BLOKE.

BLOKE: Alright?

LIAM: Alright.

BLOKE: Toilet still–

LIAM: Blocked, yeah.

BLOKE: Hideous.

LIAM: No one ever owned up—

BLOKE: It was my cousin.

LIAM: Shit.

BLOKE: Exactly... (*He looks at ALEX*) You done?

ALEX: (*painfully out of touch*) Oh. Erm, yes... Right you are... bro.

BLOKE makes his way to the cubicle. ALEX stands at the other side of the bathroom, awkwardly.

LIAM looks at his phone, calmly. We hear the noise of the piss, it's excruciatingly long.

Eventually BLOKE finishes. He stares at ALEX, intensely. He whispers something to LIAM. LIAM nods.

LIAM: (*to ALEX*) He wants to know what you're wearing around your neck.

ALEX: Oh. Erm. It's a cravat.

LIAM and BLOKE both look at each other, confused.

Like a tie, but... French.

LIAM whispers back in BLOKE's ear. They both laugh.

ALEX starts laughing along.

LIAM and BLOKE stop laughing.

BLOKE fist bumps LIAM, shakes his head, and then exits.

ALEX: Who in the hell was that?

LIAM gets his baggie out.

LIAM: I don't know. You want a key?

ALEX: You don't know him?

LIAM: Well, I mean everyone knows everyone 'round here. I don't know know him, you know? But I think maybe he's my mate's brother's mate's cousin's... mate. But, then again, I'm not 100% sure.

ALEX: Well whoever he was, he was a weirdo.

LIAM: A weirdo? You're the one wearing a cravat to a pub.

ALEX: I wanted to look my best. To dress appropriately. It's an important day. Oh, shit, bugger, blast. It is an important day. What's the time? (*ALEX checks his phone*) She'll be here in a minute.

LIAM: Who? She's coming into the gents?

ALEX: 'Here', as in, the pub. Look, I don't mean to be rude, mate, but can you leave so I can, you know, 'finish what I started' so to speak.

LIAM: Leave? Why would I wanna leave? Have you seen out there? It's horrible. Famine... war... drugs.

ALEX: *You're* on drugs.

LIAM: Cocaine doesn't count. It's basically just Pro-Plus on steroids... with a bit of coke.

ALEX: Look, my girlfriend's arriving any second, so can you just—

LIAM: Fine. I'll turn around. Best I can do. But seriously, this is an abomination.

ALEX's phone rings.

ALEX: Oh no.

LIAM: You're not gonna take that are you?

ALEX: What?

LIAM: First you ask me to leave, now you're taking phone calls.

ALEX picks it up.

ALEX: Hey, Bellz. Where are you?—OK, great—Yeah, I've only just got here—Yeah—bloody rail strikes—So, it's the booth just next to the pool table—Yeah, in between the strange flickering light and the weird guy who looks like Karl Marx if he'd gone wrong—you'll see it, with the champagne and the geraniums— Well, I thought I'd surprise you Bellz—No, no reason just... excited to see you—see you soon gorgeous—Bye, bye.

He ends the call.

LIAM: That 'weird guy' has a name. He's called Trev. He owns the pub.

ALEX: Not surprised.

LIAM: I'm also pretty sure he doesn't sell champagne.

ALEX: Prosecco will have to do.

LIAM: And why have you got her geraniums?

ALEX: They're her favourite. That's how you treat a woman.

LIAM laughs at ALEX meanly.

LIAM: I don't think that's how you treat a woman.

ALEX erupts.

ALEX: Oh. I'm sorry. Should I have bought her a pint... of... fucking Carlsberg? And a Packet of salt 'n' vinegar crisps? And some Nobby's nuts? Yeah? And then, I don't know, 'taken her back to mine', cracked open a bottle of Echo Falls, made her watch Mission Impossible 3, with my sparkling running commentary of how Tom Cruise always does his own stunts 'coz he's a fucking hard nut', then made a thinly veiled move, taken her upstairs for me to then fumble about with her bra, hump her for about three seconds, ask 'did you finish?', and then fall asleep? Is that what I should've done? Is it? Is it? I mean, do you even know what a fucking geranium is?

ALEX pants.

LIAM: Are you alright?

ALEX: Yes. I'm sorry. I just—I just—I just really need a piss but I can't piss because no one is letting me piss and I need to go outside but also I'm scared to go outside because, well, it's a big deal. Isn't it? You know? In here, time is still. Out there. It's the rest of my life. My future. Well, maybe I don't want to see my future yet. Maybe my future terrifies me, OK? Maybe this cravat is strangling me and maybe, just maybe, I want to do a wee first.

(Awkward pause.)

LIAM: I do know what a geranium is by the way.

ALEX: I'm sure you do. I'm sorry.

LIAM: It's that country next to France right?

ALEX looks at him.

I'm joking. It's a flower.

ALEX: Exactly. It's a flower.

LIAM: It wouldn't be my flower of choice for a lady, but it's still a very pretty flower. They blossom from spring until autumn and you can actually eat the leaves. Wouldn't recommend it. I tried them once and they taste like flannel.

ALEX: Keep talking about flowers please.

LIAM: I used to do a bit of gardening myself, so I know quite a bit about them. How often they need feeding, how to bud them, when they blossom. It's all actually quite... nice.

SCENE 2

Flashback: Gardening

Lights change. We're in Liam's grandfather's garden. Liam is staring into the distance, trying to focus. He looks younger and less wired.

GRANDAD: Liam?

Nothing.

Liam?

LIAM: Morning, Grandad.

GRANDAD: Morning? It's 12 o'clock. You said you'd start at 9.

LIAM: Yeah... I was out last night.

GRANDAD: Course you were.

LIAM: You can talk Grandad, you still got your pyjamas on.

GRANDAD: I've been up since 3.

LIAM: Why's that then? Sniffing your medication?

GRANDAD: Couldn't sleep. Had nightmares about what you might do to my garden this time.

LIAM: I'll spare the geraniums, don't worry.

GRANDAD: Can you even spell geraniums?

LIAM: Yeah. P-I-S-S O-F-F.

GRANDAD: I'll open the garage, you little bastard.

LIAM: You good though, yeah?

GRANDAD: Not really, mate. Wobbly. As usual. I bought you a pizza.

LIAM: Thanks.

GRANDAD: And there's a delivery I need you to put away.

LIAM: Wine Society?

GRANDAD: Yes... Try not to steal a bottle this time.

LIAM: I told you, it was the postman. He's an alcoholic.

GRANDAD: Dave is 10 years sober.

LIAM: Well, not anymore. Dave's had a relapse.

(Beat.)

Anyway, you wanna go for a walk around? Check what needs doing.

GRANDAD: My feet are too sore. Massive blisters. Not a nice sight. So I'm gonna have to trust you know what you're doing. Which I don't.

LIAM: I've been doing this for 5 years.

GRANDAD: And the place has never looked worse. Look around, Liam. Looks like a piss up at the garden centre.

LIAM: Well, I don't see the Robins complaining. They won't leave me alone.

GRANDAD: They're the Gardener's Friend. They don't need to be asked or persuaded or begged, they just come by their own accord. You can rely on them, they're always there...

They're beautiful, ain't they?

LIAM: They're alright, I guess.

The sound of a Robin.

GRANDAD: You hear that?

LIAM: I think so.

(Beat.)

GRANDAD: Make sure to fill the feeder too, they're beautiful but they're ravenous bastards.

LIAM: Alright.

GRANDAD: In a bit.

LIAM: In a bit... Oh, Grandad. You heard from Dad?

GRANDAD: What do you think, Liam?

SCENE 3

Cut back to the bathroom.

LIAM stares at his beer bottle. ALEX is looking into the urinal.

ALEX: OK... Well... I think I got some out. Half at least. Maybe more. I'm a glass half full kinda guy so that should do for now. Although I guess it depends if the glass is my penis or if it's the urinal in this metaphor, doesn't it? For now, let's say... the glass is the urinal.

LIAM: What do you do?

ALEX: What?

LIAM: Because you're wearing a fancy, if a bit tight, suit. You speak weird. And you've got that french... tie... thing—

ALEX: Cravat.

LIAM: Cravat. So, I'm thinking it's what? Something in the city, yeah?

ALEX: I work in advertising.

LIAM: No fucking way. That's amazing. You're one of them advert men.

ALEX: Yes, I'm an 'Advert Man'.

LIAM: With a big job in the city, a nice office with a swivel chair, a view of the shard? I bet you even have a Pret subscription.

ALEX: It makes financial sense. I work in brand management, marketing mostly with a focus on B2C engagement. Christ. Engagement. (*He checks his pocket and phone*) I really have to go.

ALEX goes to leave. LIAM steps in front of him.

LIAM: Wait. Wait. Wait. I've got this amazing idea for a new beer. I've had it ages but needed someone to trial it out on you, know? My best idea yet, I reckon.

ALEX: I'm sure it is... I don't even know your name.

LIAM: Liam.

ALEX: Right. I'm Alex

LIAM: I know.

(Beat.)

ALEX: What do you mean, you know?

LIAM: I heard your wife calling you it on the phone.

ALEX: Right. Not wife. Yet. Shit.

ALEX checks his phone.

Listen. I'm sorry, Liam, but I really don't have time to—

LIAM: Come on. Least you can do is give me feedback on my idea.

ALEX: She'll be waiting outside.

LIAM: They'll take care of her. The Old Swan is a kind and generous establishment.

ALEX: I highly doubt that.

LIAM: Come on. Dragons Den me, bro.

ALEX: Fine. Go. Be quick.

LIAM prepares himself.

LIAM: Yes! OK. Listen up. Picture this. Imagine if there was a brand of beer called 'Hair Of The Dog'. Yeah? You imagining?

ALEX: I guess.

LIAM: Advert. So a guy comes into the pub, walks up to the bar and he looks like he's had a proper rough one last night. He looks like you did the morning after Mr Chapman told you that you got an E in double science.

ALEX: Jesus.

LIAM: Exactly. Livid. So this guy walks up. He needs a pint desperately to stop him hangin'. So the barman looks at him and says... 'Hair of the Dog'?... The guy probably smiles at the barman and says, 'you know it, mate'. And then before he says anything else, the barman just starts pouring him a pint. But it ain't just any pint. You see? It's a pint of this new beer called: 'Hair of the Dog'. So the barman puts the beer in front of him, and the guy stares at it like, 'I didn't say I wanted that'. So the barman stares back at the guy, straight into his ugly hangin' mug and he says, 'yeah, you did. You said you wanted a Hair of the Dog, which is, in fact, the name of a beer in this hypothetical world we're now in. Oh, and by the way, that'll be Quid please... you cunt'. The End.

(Pause.)

Nothing? No feedback?

ALEX: It didn't really make any sense.

LIAM: Why not?

ALEX: Why would anyone call a beer 'Hair of the Dog'?

LIAM: What are you talkin' about? It's literally the perfect name.

ALEX: No, it's simply bad branding. If you call a beer 'Hair Of The Dog' then it's already limiting itself. It's basically saying: 'this is a drink you'll wanna have on a hangover but if you're sitting in the sun, relaxing or just having a good day, then this product probably isn't for you'. You're not making the consumer want to be a better person. That's the key. Think about it: who would you have drinking 'Hair of the Dog' in your advert? An overweight, toothless guy, reeking of booze with his gut hanging out of his 'Ministry of Sound' T-shirt? It doesn't work.

LIAM: You're mean when you turn into Advert Man.

ALEX: It's just feedback.

LIAM: Alright, Mr Hotshot. What amazing ideas have you got?

ALEX: I really don't need to prove myself to a man I met in a toilet.

LIAM: Yeah, you bloody do. I'm probably your target market. If you're gonna judge my excellent idea then you're gonna have to back it up with something amazing. I'm starting to doubt you even have any ideas yourself.

ALEX: I'm not rising to this.

LIAM: You must be really average at your job.

ALEX: (*snapping*) I'm not. I was actually only the second junior sales rep to win the most Innovative Ad Award.

LIAM: Congratulations. Then sell me something, Advert Man.

ALEX: It doesn't work like that.

LIAM: Show me your super power abilities.

ALEX: I'm off the clock.

LIAM: Sell me... (*LIAM looks around for something and settles on his own bag of cocaine*)

this coke.

ALEX: Well, I don't think I really need to—

LIAM: Yeah, fair enough. OK... (*he looks around again and then picks up some toilet paper from the floor*)... this toilet paper.

ALEX: Toilet paper?

LIAM: Yeah. Go on.

ALEX: It's toilet paper. It's kind of essential.

LIAM: You'd think that... but I'm more of a bidet person.

ALEX: Really?

LIAM: Yeah.

ALEX: You're a bidet person?

LIAM: I don't need toilet paper. I have that much money. In fact, I've got a mansion, a yacht and 10 huskies.

ALEX: 10?

LIAM: Yep. All with multi-coloured eyes. They're the ones that need the toilet paper actually, not me. It's dog toilet paper. (*toying with him*) Surely that's impossible to sell, even for you, no?

ALEX sighs.

ALEX: Fine. OK... dog toilet paper. (*takes time, muttering under his breath*) OK, Picture this.
Advert. You're standing on your yacht... huge yacht... superyacht. The sun is shining, glinting off the waves of some patch in the Mediterranean. You're there with the love of your life. And on that yacht too, are your 10 huskies.

LIAM: Are they looking cute?

ALEX: The cutest. They're waterski-ing of the back.

LIAM: Yeah.

ALEX: Anyway, you and the love of your life... have you got a special person, Liam?

LIAM: Not currently.

ALEX: Alright, well hypothetically you're going out with 'Janine'/

LIAM: (*proudly*) Janine?/

ALEX: Played by whichever famous influencer we can get on board.

LIAM: Nice.

ALEX: You and Janine are enjoying a few drinks, some canapes and are about to make love under the sun. When suddenly... you hear a woof. One of your beloved huskies tugs on your arm. A look of sheer panic in its eyes.

LIAM: 'What is it boy?'

ALEX: 'Mr Liam, sir... whilst you weren't looking, we helped ourselves to those canapes. Problem is... They've gone right through me.'

LIAM: 'What do you want me to do about it, boy?'

ALEX: 'We're stuck in the middle of the Mediterranean, sir and I need to... Suddenly you realise, you see the struggle in his little multi-coloured husky eyes, the beads of sweat on his little husky brow... You are moments away from a faecal disaster of Titanic proportions. What do you do? Throw them in the sea? No! The sea's a cruel mistress, you can't do that. But then... oh my God... out of nowhere, Janine pulls out the finest roll of (*he checks the roll*) 'Doggy Doggy Woof Woof' toilet paper. It glints in the hot Mediterranean sun... Your husky leaps up into your arms with joy and licks your face. And then runs off, toilet paper in his jaws. You're finally left alone to make love with your beautiful wife. The camera pans out. Then written across the glinting white tipped waves, we see: 'Doggy Doggy Woof Woof Toilet Paper: Canine out of 10 huskies approve'.

LIAM claps.

Wasn't my best pitch. Talking dogs are a little far-fetched. If you'll pardon the pun.

LIAM: You really are our friendly neighbourhood Advert Man.

ALEX: It was nice and ever so slightly weird meeting you, Liam.

They shake hands.

LIAM: Did you definitely finish pissing?

ALEX: Yes.

LIAM: You're telling me you got all of the piss out of your bladder, through your cock, past your enlarged vein, and into that urinal?

ALEX: No. I didn't say that, Paxman. But I did finish pissing.

LIAM: But you still need a piss?

ALEX: I'll hold it in.

LIAM: You realise holding it in can give you a UTI.

ALEX: I'll chance it.

LIAM: Jesus. Is that what the world is now? Full of advert-men who are so afraid of how weird their cocks are that they have to walk around with cravats on and half-emptied bladders.

ALEX: Goodbye, Liam.

LIAM: Wait.

ALEX opens the bathroom door and stares outside. A bright light illuminates him, as we hear the noises of the pub outside. LIAM stands behind him, holding a bottle.

LIAM: She there?

ALEX: Not yet. But Karl Marx just took a swig of my champagne.

LIAM: Prosecco.

(Pause.)

You're not moving?

ALEX: Seems not.

LIAM: Nervous?

ALEX: I'm fine.

LIAM: Cigarette?

ALEX: I don't smoke.

LIAM: Do you want a line?

ALEX: I'm good.

(Beat.)

LIAM: What's she like?

ALEX: What?

LIAM: Bella?

(Pause.)

ALEX: Erm... Bella is...

LIAM: You like her?

ALEX: I love her. I'm going to ask her to marry me.

LIAM: Wow. Marriage. Sounds awful.

ALEX: Scary, maybe. Like sailing into the unknown... But isn't that what's beautiful about it? You're not sailing alone.

LIAM: It'll rip your heart out. Better off without it, I say. My Mum and Dad got married. Ten years later, what did they have to show for it? A divorce, half a dog each... And me.

ALEX's phone rings again.

ALEX: Oh, God.

He picks up the phone.

Hey Bellz—you're outside?—brilliant—yeah, that's the one—sit down, relax, pour yourself a glass of champagne—prosecco—bubbly!—I think basically anything with bubbles can be referred to as 'bubbly'—It could be a bottle of fizzy water and you could—Yeah, anyway go nuts, I just went to the little boy's room—Just a wee—I'll be a minute Belzy boo.

LIAM: Bellzy Boo?

ALEX: Love you.

ALEX hangs up the phone and takes a deep breath. He looks in the mirror, determined.

LIAM: You good?

ALEX: Right. This is it, Parker. The biggest day of your little life. Liam. It was a pleasure to meet you but I hope I never see you again.

LIAM: Harsh.

ALEX: I'm going in.

ALEX walks towards the door.

LIAM: Why don't you just have—

LIAM offers a cigarette packet to ALEX.

ALEX: No!

ALEX smacks them out of LIAM's hand cinematically.

LIAM: Wow.

ALEX: I'm sorry.

LIAM: That was big. That was a very big thing you just did. You knocked my cigarettes out my hand, onto the pissy floor, covered in piss. There's probably piss on my cigarettes now. Piss.

ALEX: That was very out of character for me.

LIAM: Was it?

ALEX: I'm nervous, Liam. This is it. The moment I've been planning for months. Everything's meant to be perfect.

LIAM: You got the ring?

ALEX: Yeah, left hand pocket.

LIAM: You got the speech?

ALEX: Right hand pocket.

LIAM: You got the confidence? Which pocket is that in?

ALEX: Shit, must have left my confidence on the train. Of course I do.

LIAM: No you don't. You're a shell, mate. You're gonna crumble out there. You look ill, actually.

ALEX: I'll be fine.

LIAM: Really? Do you actually think you'll be fine? About to open your heart to the woman you love. Look, Alex, I'm going to level with you mate, I don't normally spend this length of time speaking to randoms I've just met in the toilets of this fine establishment. I don't know how, but I have this feeling that we're like... connected, man. Do you know what I mean?

ALEX: No.

LIAM: I don't mean in some weird spiritual way, but I feel like we know each other in another life. You know? Like maybe I was a dog, you were a cat, and I sniffed your arse before. You know? Look... Can I be completely honest with you?

ALEX: I don't know.

LIAM: I honestly think, hand on heart, no bull shit for a second, man to man, that you should do a bump of coke.

LIAM takes out his baggie.

ALEX: No chance. I'll be an anxious mess.

LIAM: Look at you mate, you're at peak anxiety already... This'll calm you down. Promise.

ALEX: I haven't had good experiences.

LIAM: You need it.

ALEX: What if it gives me a heart attack or, worse... what if I poo myself?

LIAM: Come on Alex, first off... What better place to poo yourself? Secondly, we're not in some 80s anti-drug advert. It'll make you feel a little more confident, that's it. It'll make you feel a little bit less... you know... like you.

(Pause.)

ALEX: Alright. Give me a bump.

LIAM: Here we go.

ALEX: Bump me up. Bump me up, Scotty.

LIAM gives ALEX a bump of coke from his key. ALEX snorts it passionately.

SCENE 4

Flashback: Work

Lights change. MR PREECE's office - ALEX's boss. MR PREECE is stood, waiting. ALEX enters.

MR PREECE: Alex Parker.

ALEX: Mr Preece, you said you wanted to see me?

MR PREECE: Yes. I'm afraid so.

ALEX: Right?

MR PREECE: I'm afraid you're just not cutting the mustard, Alex. I'm going to have to let you go.

ALEX: What? Are you serious?

MR PREECE: There isn't room for error. Not even an inch. You've got to let the best rise to the top of the golden elevator, and the worst drop from the tree. Do you agree?

ALEX: But but I've been here for—

MR PREECE: Collect your things and be on your way.

ALEX: I... erm.. OK.

ALEX is distraught, he goes to leave.

MR PREECE: Alex?

ALEX: Yes, sir.

MR PREECE: I hate to ask you a difficult question at a time like this. But, why does it say 'I'm a gullible piece of shit' on your forehead.

ALEX: Oh.

MR PREECE erupts with laughter.

MR PREECE: I'm messing with you! Your face. 'You've got to let the best rise to the top of the golden elevator, and the worst drop from the tree'... that doesn't even make sense as a metaphor. It's contrived.

ALEX: Good one, Mr Preece. Top quality.

MR PREECE: Listen, let's cut the horse shit, I do actually want to speak to you about your performance. You've been by far our best salesmen in this team for the last few months. And, not only that, you've had the best ideas. Your 'Player Pack Attack' campaign won this year's Most Innovative Ad Award. You want to know the last Junior Sales Rep that won that award?

ALEX: You.

MR PREECE: Me. Yes. How did you know?

ALEX: Well, it's on the bottom of all company emails.

MR PREECE: Yes.

ALEX: And on that plaque above your desk.

MR PREECE: Yes.

ALEX: And it's even written on the urinal cakes.

MR PREECE: Best five grand I ever spent.

PREECE smiles.

My hope was that it would one day inspire a young buck like you and, by God, it has. You're a good kid Alex Parker. I was right to trust your father's recommendation. He spoke very highly of you. I know some won't agree, but for me, you can always trust nepotism. I feel like we've got a good dynamic betwixt us. You're a stormtrooper. And I'm Anakin... post-op... You feel?

ALEX: Yeah?

MR PREECE: I want to promote you. You'll be in charge of a small team I'm putting together for our most recent client. Bet Time.

ALEX: Bedtime?

MR PREECE: Bet Time. With a T. They're a new up and coming gambling website. Their aim is to redefine the world of gambling. Make it easier, more accessible, more addictive. They want to do something that really stands out. Any thoughts?

ALEX: OK. OK.

ALEX paces before looking out the window.

Look out there. Life is... boring. Unbelievably boring. You're in a dead-end job, you work overtime and you can barely pay your rent. You're lonely too, because you haven't got the energy that's required to give to a meaningful relationship. You spend most of your days tired. So tired. Too tired to bother with cooking, too tired to read, too tired to watch anything that lasts longer than 30 minutes. In fact, most days, the best you can muster is lifting up your phone to your face and endlessly scrolling until you eventually just pass out. But wait... it's not time to sleep. No. It's time to wake up.

MR PREECE makes an alarm sound effect.

ALEX: That's right, It's not bedtime. It's Bet Time. A place where you can bet on anything at any time and all with just the press of a button. You can bet on the Football, the Basketball, even the Rugby... ball. You can bet in-play, out of play, any kind of play you like.

MR PREECE: I was wondering how many seconds this pitch might last?

ALEX: Well, there's a bet for that too. Because with Bet Time, we make sure it's easy. The easiest thing you've ever done. Leave the hard stuff to life. And with approachable, friendly, 24/7 chat advisers, all too eager to help you place your bets, explain the odds, or even just a nice conversation. We've got you. We understand you. Because isn't life that little bit more exciting when there's something to win... especially when you've nothing to lose? So come on. Wake up. It's...

MR PREECE: Bet Time... Nice. I knew I could trust you, Alex. Run with it.

(Beat.)

Oh, and there's a tasty little bonus in it for you too. Maybe you can finally buy that ring for your girlfriend.

ALEX: Ring?

MR PREECE: Everyone in this building knows you've been planning to propose for months.

ALEX: Really?

MR PREECE: So, what do you reckon? You wanna move to the next level? It's lonely up here at the top.

They shake hands.

SCENE 5

Cut back to the bathroom.

ALEX is staring into the mirror, panting. The cocaine has kicked in.

ALEX: Can I try out my speech on you?

LIAM: Speech?

ALEX: Because, you know, you can give me feedback. Like I did with your shit 'Hair of the Dog' beer idea, you know? I want feedback!

LIAM: Alright.

ALEX: Then maybe you can tell me, you know, if it's going to go well or if it's going to go badly. It's going to go perfectly!

LIAM: OK.

ALEX: Good.

LIAM: So, I'm Bella, right?

ALEX: What!?

LIAM: In this imagined situation?

ALEX: Of course you're fucking Bella! Who else would you be!?

LIAM: Relax, Advert Man!

ALEX: I am relaxed!

LIAM: Go on then.

ALEX: OK...

ALEX takes out a piece of paper and begins to read, very quickly.

Bella.

LIAM: Yes.

ALEX: I have a complex set of feelings for you.

LIAM: OK.

ALEX: I have a complex set of feelings for you, and I think that the conditions of our lives are now perfect for us to go to the next level in our relationship. A window has been opened, metaphorically. We started dating, and then about one month later I asked you to be my girlfriend, and then six months later we moved in together and now, two years later, with my job and your job both at critical career points, it seems only sensical to become one... in a matrimonial way.

LIAM: OK...

ALEX: Isabelle Bronwyn Cecilia Houghton-Houseman?

LIAM: Christ.

ALEX: Isabelle Bronwyn Cecilia Houghton-Houseman!

LIAM: Yes.

ALEX: Will you do me the logical gesture of becoming my wife?

LIAM: No.

ALEX: What?

LIAM: That was horrible.

ALEX: Was it?

LIAM: You're supposed to work in advertising.

ALEX: I do.

LIAM: You had no soul at all, man. You sounded like if Mark Zuckerberg and a Tamagotchi had a kid, and that kid tried to propose to a brick.

ALEX's phone rings. ALEX looks at it and answers it defiantly.

ALEX: Hold on, Bella, I'll be out in a mo, I'm doing a poo.

He hangs up.

LIAM: And now she's gonna be thinking of you doing a poo.

ALEX: Oh God.

LIAM: No offence mate, but if I were Bella... Bella... Donna... Bindweed or whatever, I'd be sick on myself and leave the pub in floods of tears if you said all of that to me. No, I'd slap you first, hard, then be sick on myself and then I'd leave in floods of tears.

ALEX: I get it. So what? I need to make a few quick edits? That's do-able. But quickly. Quickly!

LIAM: You need to speak from the heart. Lose the paper.

ALEX: You're right. You're so right. OK. From the heart. Lose the paper.

ALEX crumples up the paper and puts it in his mouth.

LIAM: Don't eat it.

ALEX spits it out.

Let's start this again. OK? I'll be Bella. Remember. I'm your girlfriend and you love me and you want to spend the rest of your life with me. Forever. Kids. Dog. Spaghetti Bolognese on Sundays. The lot.

ALEX: Right. Of course.

LIAM: You want to make me feel like you care about me. Like you wouldn't want to look at anyone else.

ALEX: Yes.

LIAM: Like you won the lottery when you met me.

ALEX: I know exactly what you mean.

LIAM: Little bump of 'Pro-Plus' before we go again?

ALEX nods. LIAM aeroplanes a key of coke into ALEX's nostril and then does one himself.

Alright. Let me start this time.

ALEX stands, pretending to be BELLA.

(*American accent*) Hey, Alex. So lovely of you to finally show. I was thinking of actually eating these geraniums. I was so bored. Did you know that they were actually edible? Liam told me. He's very handsome. And tall. And sensitive.

ALEX: Listen here... randomly American version of Bella, put those geraniums away. I've got something to say.

LIAM: Oh yeah?

ALEX: Oh yeah, oh yeah, oh yeah. I love you. Because... because... Because you're it, Bellz.

LIAM: Yeah?

ALEX: Yeah, you, you, you are IT. Hell, you're it and everything. You're more than words can even express.

(*Beat.*)

LIAM: Why don't you sing it?

ALEX: What?

LIAM: Sing it.

ALEX: OK... you sure?

LIAM: Certain.

ALEX starts to sing 'More Than a Woman'. At first it is barely audible but then he becomes more and more confident as the song progresses.

ALEX: (*sung*) Oh, girl, I've known you very well. I've seen you growing every day. I never really looked before. But now you take my breath away. Suddenly you're in my life, part of everything I do. You got me working day and night. Just tryin' to keep a hold on you. Here in your arms I found my paradise. My only chance for happiness. And if I lose you now, I think I would die. Oh, say you'll always be my baby, we can make it shine. We can take forever, just a minute at a time. More than a woman. More than a woman to me.

32

ALEX suddenly clutches his chest.

My heart... It feels like it's about to burst.

LIAM: (*still with an American accent*) That's so sweet.

ALEX: No genuinely. I think I'm having a heart attack.

ALEX falls to the floor.

Liam, do something.

LIAM does nothing.

Liam, help me.

LIAM does nothing.

Please.

LIAM suddenly awakens.

LIAM: Sorry. Yeah.

ALEX: Why are you just standing there?

LIAM: What do I do?

ALEX: Get Bella.

LIAM: OK. Give me your phone.

ALEX: Don't call her. Go get her.

LIAM: OK. OK. Drink this, alright?

LIAM passes him the beer.

It's gonna be fine, mate. It'll pass.

LIAM exits.

SCENE 6

Flashback: ALEX's FATHER

Lights change. ALEX sits in his bedroom. ALEX's FATHER enters.

FATHER: You have me for 10 minutes, Alex. That's all. I've got golf at one and the bunker is well and truly calling my name. (*He laughs to himself, but notices ALEX sitting on the floor*) What is it you wanted to talk about?

ALEX stands up.

ALEX: I'm thinking about a career change, Dad.

FATHER: Ah. This again. This feels like more of a 15 minute conversation, no?

ALEX: It's a step up.

FATHER: You truly believe moving to Africa and playing with elephants is a step up?

ALEX: It's a step somewhere.

FATHER: A step away, no?

(Beat.)

ALEX: They're an NGO, a Non-Government Organisation.

FATHER: I know what an NGO is.

ALEX: Sorry. It's a company called Solar Aid. They work on delivering solar panels in African countries. Renewable energy.

FATHER: Renewable energy?

ALEX: It's the future.

FATHER: (*sarcastically*) Wow, 'the future.' What about your future? What about Isabelle?

ALEX: She'll understand.

FATHER: Have you proposed to her yet?

ALEX: I truly believe this is a great opportunity for me. I'd be working on their ad campaign, using my experience, trying to get funding from big businesses-

FATHER: And what about your job? The job that I got you. The job that I had to persuade them to let you have, that I put my neck on the line for. What about that?

ALEX: I'm thankful for that... but I don't exactly find it—

FATHER: They are a reputable company, Alex!

ALEX: I'm not sure I want to work there anymore, Dad.

(Beat.)

FATHER: Is this about—

ALEX: No.

FATHER: Jesus, Alex. You've got to grow thicker skin.

ALEX: It's not about that—

FATHER: A kid died. Move on. Kids die all the time. I'm sure a few kids have died putting up those solar panels you're on about. Listen to me, Alex. Stick with it. Your mother and I didn't spend thousands of pounds on your tuition for you to go prancing about in the desert. Show me that you are actually built for this world.

ALEX: I am.

FATHER: You are what?

ALEX: I am built for this world.

FATHER: Then prove it, Alex.

(Pause.)

Your life is in your hands.

SCENE 7

Cut back to the bathroom.

TAMBALA music plays. ALEX is sitting against the wall, sipping beer. His heart is beating slower than it was.

After a while LIAM returns.

LIAM: You alright?

ALEX: I'm not dead. Is she coming?

LIAM: Erm...

ALEX: What? Is she OK?

LIAM: She wasn't there.

ALEX: What?

LIAM: She left.

ALEX: How do you know?

LIAM: My mates saw her leave. They said she looked pretty angry.

ALEX: I need to call her—

LIAM: Let me do it.

ALEX's phone lies in the middle of the stage, from when he fell over previously. LIAM takes it.

LIAM: Password?

ALEX: 'BellzyBoo'... With a Z.

LIAM: Ah... mate.

ALEX: What?

LIAM: She's just texted you.

ALEX: What did she say?

LIAM: ' Well done. You not only succeeded at taking me to the worst pub in this entire city, The Old Swan, but also at not turning up at all. I'll see you back at my parents. I'm not sure about this anymore... P.S: you're a twat.'

ALEX: Oh... right.

LIAM: I added the last bit, but yeah, she's gone, mate.

ALEX: That's it then, It's all ruined. Everything. Oh, God.

ALEX slumps into himself. He begins to cry.

LIAM: Hey. Let her leave. You can come back to mine, if ya want? We can finish off this baggie together. Keep chatting. We could even crack open a bottle of Echo Falls.

ALEX looks up at LIAM.

Watch Mission Impossible 3? Did you know Tom Cruise did his own stunts?

ALEX starts to laugh.

See. There ya go.

ALEX continues to laugh hysterically.

ALEX: You're funny, Liam.

LIAM: Thanks.

ALEX: You're bloody hilarious... You think I want to chat to you? You actually think I want to stay here and talk to you? It's your fucking fault my proposal's gone to shit.

LIAM: You're the one still in this toilet.

ALEX: You think that's out of choice, Liam? Why would anyone want to be stuck in here with you? I mean, have you even got any friends?

LIAM: Yeah.

ALEX: And where are they, Liam?

LIAM: Out there.

ALEX: Out there? Wait. On the big table? Those were your mates? I heard them when I first arrived. Laughing their heads off. I think the entire pub heard them. So they were laughing at you. It was you they were calling an idiot. Telling you to get off your phone. Telling you to stop using mildly offensive jokes to mask the fact that you have nothing interesting to say. Let me just make sure, ***those*** were your mates?

LIAM: Yep.

LIAM does a key of coke.

ALEX: Because from what I can gather you've just spent about 30 minutes doing coke and talking about piss with a complete stranger. A complete stranger who, funnily enough, thinks that you are a cunt. So, seriously, Liam. I need a little bit more help here because I'm really struggling. I'm struggling like I was that day in Double Science, remember? Remember that made-up circumstance you invented so I'd speak to you. So please, you need to enlighten me, Liam. Where are your actual mates?

LIAM: I have actual mates.

ALEX: Name one.

LIAM: John.

ALEX: And who's John?

(Pause.)

LIAM: He somehow got himself to uni, and now he's doing a dumb job up in the city. Like the rest of them. Like you. But he loves doing standup. You know, standup comedy. And you know what? He's actually pretty funny. Mean. But funny. But I guess that's comedy for you. Ain't it? And he's getting better at it 'cos he cares. You can tell he really cares. He does open mic nights, he watches 8 Out of 10 Cats... and he's started a TikTok account, which... I dunno... I guess that shows he's for real. But you know what the mad thing is, Alex?

ALEX: What?

LIAM: He gets this crazy glint in his eye when he talks about it. Like he's on it. It's the exact same look my other mate Sam gets when he speaks about corporate finance. Or you, when you turn into Advert Man.

ALEX: It's called passion, Liam.

LIAM: Passion? Well then they're all full of it. I'll be sitting around the table with all of the boys and something will come up. Something... 'topical'? That's the word. Something they all wanna debate. Like the death penalty, poverty or Boris Johnson. And you can tell it's gonna happen because someone will put a different voice on. This weird... adult voice. A 'nah let's stop fucking about for a second boys' voice. And then it'll begin. They'll chat and chat, and use words I don't understand like... 'contemplate' and 'berate' and 'Overton Window'... I mean who the fuck is Overton anyway? Didn't he play for Newcastle?

(Beat.)

LIAM: At first it would just be one of them. Testing the waters after first year of uni. Taking the plunge. Someone would say: 'what do you boys think about Ebola?', and then another would say: 'Yeah... it's a weird one'. And that would be it. It wouldn't go very far. But now all of them do it. Even fucking John. He doesn't know much either but he's always got something jokes to say. A one liner, like: 'who the fuck is Overton anyway? Didn't he play for Newcastle?'. Yep. That wasn't me. He came up with that one.

ALEX: Right.

LIAM: But me? When I hear that weird voice start to buzz in each of their mouths I just get my phone out. Go for a gret, get a pint, do a line, speak to Trev, literally anything to avoid being dragged into it. Because, I'm not gonna lie to you mate, I don't know what they're talking about. I never got the memo in the post about us needing to do homework before meeting up for a beer. We used to play drinking games, Fifa, get with girls... Not sit in a pub with no music and chat about the price of plastic bags. And I'll see it. That glint in each of their eyes, as they give their opinions and use their big words. And I'll realise that I haven't spoken in about 10 minutes, but it feels like 4 hours, and slowly they'll all clock on. One by one like fucking dominos. Glancing at me. The energy all on me. As I stare down at my phone... Then... everytime... almost like in slow motion... one of them... usually John... Nah, always fucking John... will take a sip from his pint... place it down on the table... wipe a bit of leftover beer off his pubey beard... wipe the beer from his hand onto his trousers... he'll clear his throat... smile... and he'll say... 'Oi Liam... let me get a word in'.

(Beat.)

And it's funny. Course it's funny. I mean I haven't spoken in a while, fair play. I get it. Everyone gets it. So I look up and smile. Like I've just been caught having a wank. 'Nice one John'.

(Beat.)

But you know what I wanna do sometimes? Sometimes... I wanna wait till John asks me for another line, a line he hasn't paid for cos he 'doesn't like that stuff'. And we'll go into the toilet, like best mates sharing a secret, and I'll rack him up a big one. And he'll lean over, his eyes fixed on the prize and... I'll take one of my cubicle beers... and smash it down on something hard... Like the back of his skull... Blood covering him as that smirk is wiped off his face. And then, you know what I'd do?

ALEX: What?

LIAM: I'd stand over him, lying on the pissy floor. And say, 'you know what, mate... I will get a word in. Maybe they won't be big words like you lot with your degrees and jobs up in Farringdon, and maybe I won't get a glint in my eye when I talk about Boris, or the Himalayas or about whether porn is or is not psychologically damaging. And maybe I can't stand up in front of people and do shit jokes like you, John. But you know what I do care about? Do you know when I do get a glint in my eye, mate? You know when I do get passionate? When I get fucked. When I do this (*he holds up the baggie of coke*). I love it more than any of you will ever love anything. And you all join me on the train of joy for a bit... for a few stops, then you'll jump off again and go back to your boring lives. But I'm on it for life. And when I'm on it, I have that glint in every part of my body. Everywhere. And when I'm on it... I'm me. I'm honest. I'm nice. I'm chatty. I'm the guy everyone wants to talk to at the pub. I'm the guy all the girls want to speak to. So I hope you enjoy your 10 seconds of fame John. I do. 'Cos I'm about to have another line. And when I go back. You know what's gonna happen? You boys are all gonna love me again'.

SCENE 8

Flashback: LIAM's DAD

Lights change. Living room. LIAM's DAD is sitting watching TV. LIAM enters.

DAD: Incredible.

LIAM enters.

LIAM: Dad.

LIAM's DAD doesn't respond.

Not at Kate's tonight?

LIAM's DAD shrugs. He sips his beer.

What you watching?

DAD: Catch a Killer. Crime doc. Re-run.

LIAM: I went to the hospital. Saw Grandad. He... well, he probably didn't realise I was there, but he seemed happy to have a visitor, you know? Kept banging on about the Robins. I told him I'd keep the feeder full.

DAD: (*pointing at the TV*) You see Liam... This guy here, he's smart. He's made it look like that one's the murderer, by getting himself all beat up so he looks like the victim, when actually he did it all along.

LIAM sits down next to his DAD.

LIAM: Nice.

DAD: (*to the TV*) It was him. Check the fingerprints. They never learn.

LIAM gets his phone out and starts gambling.

LIAM: Yeah.

DAD: How are you affording that? You're unemployed ain't ya?

LIAM: Got a loan. Watch this.

LIAM shows him his phone.

100 on red.

DAD: It was black.

LIAM: Yeah. But now look. 200 on red.

DAD: (*to the TV*) Check the CCTV!

LIAM: Dad, look.

DAD: (*to the TV*) That bloke saw the whole thing but he's keeping quiet.

LIAM: It's a system. It can only ever be red or black, right? That's why it's just so fucking fantastic. So you bet on red with a 100. You lose. Fine. It happens. So rather than walk away like an idiot you bet on red again with £200. Double it up. But you lose again. So now you've lost £300. So what do you do?

DAD: (*to the TV*) It's obviously him.

LIAM: You double it again. £400. And you... Go on, press it.

LIAM's DAD ignores him. LIAM presses it himself.

DAD: (*to the TV*) This detective, she knows. The rest of you are clueless.

LIAM: You lose again. Shit. £700 lost. Time to walk away?

DAD: Any more beers in the fridge?

LIAM: You bet again, double. £800. And guess what?

DAD: (*to the TV*) He's not seriously going to get away with it?

LIAM: Watch Dad.

LIAM presses the button. He wins. His DAD laughs at the TV.

DAD: (*to the TV*) He's one lucky fucker.

LIAM: You win 1600 quid. Obviously, you've spent 100, 200, 400, 800... 1500 quid. So 100 pound profit. And that's how it works: it's called the Martingale System.

DAD: (*to the TV*) Was it really worth the risk?

LIAM: It has to land on red eventually.

SCENE 9

Cutback to the bathroom.

LIAM and ALEX are sitting next to each other, mirroring the scene just gone.

LIAM does a bump of coke. A new lease of life. He hands ALEX the bag.

LIAM: You know something, I know I'm not the best company in the world. But she's gonna be annoyed at you anyway. What have you got to lose? Nothing to be gained tonight. You might as well have a chat, go home, sort it out in the morning.

ALEX: I'm a coward. I'd rather stay in this disgusting toilet than go out there and tell the girl I love that I want to marry her.

LIAM: Come on. Cheer up. What have you got to be sad about? You're the model man. You've got a job. You're making tons. You've almost got a wife.

ALEX: Almost.

LIAM: And you like your job.

ALEX: It's alright.

LIAM: Well, there you go. It's alright. At least you're not miserable.

ALEX: But I don't wanna settle for 'alright'. I'm sick of people saying they're lives aren't the way they want them to be, but not doing anything about it. It's pathetic. It makes me sick. Get up and do something. You know?

LIAM: Well, I'm in awe of you, mate. Everything you do. How you can make someone want something that they don't even need. Maybe even something that they shouldn't need, you know? Like dog-toilet paper.

ALEX: It's not always as fun as dog toilet paper.

LIAM: What are you working on at the moment?

ALEX: I've been working on a project called Bet Time.

LIAM: The gambling site?

ALEX: Yeah.

LIAM: Think I've heard of it.

ALEX: Yeah? It's good money.

LIAM: Do you gamble?

ALEX: God no.

LIAM: I buy a £1 scratch card from time to time. Won £20 quid once.

ALEX: Do yourself a favour, Liam. Don't bother.

LIAM: I think it's fun. Poker, roulette, scratch cards. It raises the stakes, you know? Makes life a little more exciting.

ALEX: That's how they get you.

LIAM: Do you ever feel guilty?

ALEX: Huh?

LIAM: Working for a gambling company.

ALEX: I don't know what you mean?

LIAM: You don't actually play it yourself. You know it leads to people losing a lot of money. Yet you use all your superpower Advert Man abilities to make them want to carry on. Doesn't that ever make you feel bad?

ALEX: No. You have to feel a sense of detachment, don't you? The world is what it is. It's not my fault if someone's had to remortgage their house because they've got addicted to Candy Crush.

LIAM: Do you really believe that?

ALEX: I work for an advertising agency. It's my job, I advertise, I sell what they tell me to sell. It's just clients and consumers. There's no point overthinking it.

(Pause.)

I once worked on a campaign for a football games company, where kids would unlock new players through packs they'd open. It was potluck, but obviously it wasn't, the company made sure that every 1 in 5 was programmed to be good... well, good enough. And my campaign made sure that those kids believed that they were one more pack away from Messi or whoever.

So they'd try and unlock more and more and of course, very quickly they run out of free packs and then you have to pay, but these kids are in deep, they think they're so close... so who do they turn to? The bank of Mum and Dad. It was a hit. The parents couldn't help but fund it. The company was so happy they gave us all bonuses.

LIAM: And what about the parents that couldn't?

ALEX: I mean some stories started to trickle through: Articles, screenshots. Apparently one kid had stolen his mum's card, owed us £8,000 and his mum couldn't afford it... Andy. His name was Andy. His mum went to the papers. This kid felt so guilty that he... (*beat*)... He was only 13, but then again, I was only 22.

LIAM: Right.

ALEX: Between you and me, Liam, I wouldn't let my kids go anywhere near that stuff. I blame the parents. It comes from this desire for dopamine. That feeling you get when you win after holding out for just long enough. But you can get that feeling from anything, a hug, spaghetti bolognaise, just some encouragement for god's sake. But oh yeah, (*sarcastic*) we offer an alternative and we're the bad guys. But there wouldn't be any need for that alternative if these people's lives weren't so fucking boring and miserable. God I've missed coke.

LIAM looks at the empty bag.

LIAM: You finished it.

ALEX: Well, there you go. I didn't have a heart attack after all, eh?

LIAM: You finished all of it.

ALEX: We finished all of it.

LIAM: What if you don't get that hug? What if you can't change the fact that your life's just so boring and miserable?

ALEX: You think I ever got hugged, Liam? The most my father ever gave me was a gentle pat on the back. Your life is in your hands. Unless you're born with arms for legs or.. eyes that slowly eat themselves. But even then, join a circus. Get a TikTok account.

LIAM: John had a TikTok account.

ALEX: You said... (*ALEX stretches*) You know what? I'm feeling better. I think it's time I faced the music, can't keep hiding in here forever. Can I have my phone back?

LIAM doesn't respond.

Liam?

LIAM: I'll bet you for it.

ALEX: I'm fine, thanks.

LIAM: Go on. Are you gonna spend the rest of your life advertising something you don't even understand?

ALEX: It's my phone. Why the hell would I bet you for it? It's mine.

LIAM: Oh my God. Just live a little you boring, canary wharf, tight-suited, emotionless cunt.

(Silence.)

ALEX: What have you got to bet?

LIAM: I'll bet my phone.

ALEX: Your cracked brick vs my new iPhone?

LIAM: Think about all the bumps I've given you.

ALEX: I thought... you said... Fine... Alright, deal.

LIAM gets out a coin.

LIAM: Heads or tails?

ALEX: Heads.

LIAM flips the coin. He doesn't show ALEX which side the coin has landed on.

LIAM: Heads.

ALEX: Keep your phone. Give me mine.

LIAM: Double or nothing.

ALEX: What?

LIAM: My phone and my shoes vs your phone.

ALEX: Still not even.

LIAM: Heads or tails?

ALEX: Heads

LIAM flips coin.

LIAM: Heads again.

ALEX: Liam, give me my phone.

LIAM: Double or nothing again.

ALEX: No. This is ridiculous.

LIAM: Phone, shoes and... my wallet.

ALEX: It's empty.

LIAM flips the coin. He looks at ALEX. ALEX sighs.

Fine. Tails.

LIAM: Tails. You lucky bastard.

ALEX: Give me my phone.

LIAM: : Doubl—

ALEX: I said no..

LIAM: Alright. Take it all.

LIAM passes his stuff over. ALEX grabs his phone back and reluctantly looks at LIAM's possessions.

ALEX: I really don't need these.

LIAM: A bet's a bet. All's fair in love and gambling. Just take them.

ALEX: You're a strange man, Liam.

LIAM: At least I don't con people. Anyway, go on. You best go. Life to lead, people to meet, woman to marry.

ALEX looks through his phone.

ALEX: Jesus christ. 16 texts, 15 missed calls and 3 voicemails from Bella... What's going on, Liam?

LIAM: What are you referring to, Alex?

ALEX: I'm referring to the fact that Bella only left 5 minutes ago. She was in this pub waiting. Which means she wasn't gone when you checked.

LIAM: Must've missed her.

ALEX: And she never sent that text. The text that you said she sent.

LIAM: Must've misread it.

ALEX: Another way of getting me to stay? Pretending my girlfriend had gone? Pretending you'd tried to find her? What if I had an actual heart attack you piece of shit?

LIAM: What if you had had a heart attack on one bump of coke?

ALEX: Well yes, what if I had?

LIAM: Then you would have done the world a massive favour, Alex Parker. Alex Parker from Bet Time. A company that has single handedly taken 18 thousands pounds from my bank account in the last six months.

ALEX takes a moment.

ALEX: Is that what this has all been about? Jesus, you're pathetic.

LIAM: I'm pathetic?

ALEX: Yes, Liam. If you've got a problem, I'm sorry. I really am. But fix yourself.

LIAM: I did. I stopped. I asked to be self-excluded. To be taken off the site, blocked or whatever. I called up. Spoke to a woman called Lianne. She said, yeah. No worries. I'll do that for you. Then, one night, after a gram, I was hovering over the website and a little man, with greased back hair and a shutterstock smile popped up on the chat and said 'Hello Liam, how can I help you?'. And I told him, 'thanks, but you can't mate, cos I'm trying not to gamble anymore'. And he asked me why that was. And I told him because I'd lost 5k on roulette and didn't have any left. Do you know what he said? He said that 'payday loan services allow you to get money fast', he said 'if you're running low on cash, use that as a way to win it back'. So what do you think I did? I took his advice, high as a kite on dopamine, or whatever. And I lost more money than I ever had before that night.

ALEX: Liam—

LIAM: 600% APR... And I can't make a single fucking payment.

ALEX: I know it's not fair, but that's nothing to do with Bet Time.

LIAM: But, here's the funny bit *(he laughs)*... Do you know what the guy was called?

ALEX: What?

LIAM: Do you know what that little man who popped up that night and forced me into the fucking mountain of debt that I'm in right now was called? His name was Alex.

ALEX: *(genuine confusion)* What?

LIAM: And it didn't take me long to find you, Alex... Alex Parker from Bet Time. You post a lot on LinkedIn, don't you? You posted that you were heading out here for a little getaway with your girlfriend. Bella. Bella Houseman. She went to the private girl's school here. I remember her. She was always very boring. So I thought, what better opportunity to finally meet you? To finally come face to face with the man who put me here.

ALEX moves to the door. LIAM blocks his path.

ALEX: You're insane.

LIAM: I wanted to see what you were like.

ALEX: And do what?

LIAM: I don't know. I didn't think that far ahead to be honest.

ALEX: Liam. You're evidently unhinged, OK. And I'm sorry that you happen to be one of the suckers that gambling sites seem to prey on. I am. I honestly am. But, do you really think that I work as a chat-person? It's a bot, or something. I'm not going to be working at 3 am, am I? I mean you were probably speaking to some bloke from Vietnam that they gave the name of Alex to so people like you would find them more relatable.

LIAM pushes ALEX up against the wall.

LIAM: It was you. Don't lie.

ALEX: How could it be? I work for an advertising agency. Bet Time is one of our clients. Do you understand that? And besides, Bet Time has a very strict policy on addiction prevention. If anyone had been persuading you to use payday loans, which to me sounds practically impossible, the chat would have been instantly red flagged.

LIAM: You think I'm lying?

LIAM throws ALEX to the ground.

ALEX: I think you're a sad man, Liam. I think you're a sad man who's lost a lot in life but doesn't quite know how to bring things back, but I can't help you. Read a book or something, listen to a podcast, make your bed. Do anything. Because right now, you're not a fun person for anyone to be around.

LIAM: I bet I've had more fun doing a bag of this, than you've had in your entire life.

ALEX: Well, there you go. It was a pleasure, Liam. Really.

ALEX goes to give back the shoes, wallet and phone to LIAM.

Have these back.

LIAM: No. Keep them. You won them.

ALEX: Whatever. Well, look, here's a 50 at least. Why don't you buy yourself another gram, yeah?

ALEX drinks the last bit of beer from the bottle, leaves it on the side, and then drops a 50 pound note on the floor. He exits.

LIAM is left alone. No shoes. No phone. No wallet. He stares at the 50 pound note. He eventually picks it up. He then looks at the beer on the floor.

For a moment, he hears the sound of a Robin. He smiles. The sound stops.

After a moment, LIAM slowly walks towards the cubicle and opens the door.

He drags out a body. All we can see is the legs. Not moving. JOHN's.

LIAM takes a phone from JOHN's pocket. It has blood on it. He dials a number.

LIAM: (*emotional*) Hello—Hello?—Hi—police please—Yeah, my mate, John. He's not breathing and he's bleeding... a lot—He's been hit—Yeah, sorry—Toilet's at the Old Swan—There was a guy, in a cravat—I think he was on something—My phone, my wallet, my trainers. He took them—Yeah. Sorry. We've both been hit—A bottle—yeah—come quick please—John isn't breathing.

ALEX hangs up. He drops the phone on the floor.

He licks any cocaine out of the bag.

He takes the beer bottle, raises it in the air, mirroring the image at the beginning of the play. He takes a deep breath, and smashes it over his head.

Blackout.

'More Than A Woman' by Tambala plays. We hear the sound of sirens.

THE END.

ALSO AVAILABLE FROM SALAMANDER STREET

All Salamander Street plays can be bought in bulk at a discount for performance or study. Contact info@salamanderstreet.com to enquire about performance licenses.

I LOST MY VIRGINITY TO CHOPIN'S NOCTURNE IN B-FLAT MINOR by Sebastian Gardner
ISBN: 9781914228162

A bittersweet comedy which focuses on the disparity between classes and how much of your self identity you would comprise for someone you love.

STEVE AND TOBIAS VERSUS DEATH
by Sebastian Gardner & Daniel Kettle
ISBN: 9781914228872

This throat-ripping zombie comedy pits the gore of horror against the hysterical instability of family life.

ALGORITHMS by Sadie Clark
ISBN: 9781738429394

A bisexual Bridget Jones for the online generation.

THE LAST TEMPTATION OF BORIS JOHNSON
by Jonathan Maitland
ISBN: 9781913630768

It was the dinner that changed history: the night in February 2016 when Boris Johnson decided to vote 'leave' and a nation's future was sealed.

COWBOYS AND LESBIANS by Billie Esplen
ISBN: 9781914228902

Charming, queer romantic comedy about British schoolfriends writing a parody American coming-of-age romance.

www.ingramcontent.com/pod-product-compliance
Lightning Source LLC
Chambersburg PA
CBHW070012100426
42741CB00012B/3208